Contents

Acknowledgements   2

I. Introduction   5

II. Method   7

III. Summary of Research Literature   9

IV. Summary of Key Findings   21

V. Conclusions: Towards Evidence Based Practice   31

References   35

Appendix – Sample Measures   40

    Measure 1:   Multiple Choice Knowledge – Guidelines &
                  Questionnaire

    Measure 2:   Confidence Scale

    Measure 3:   Training Feedback Form

    Measure 4:   Assessing Competence in Physical Skills

    Measure 5:   Measuring Direct Training Outcomes

I. Introduction

This document is part of a series of initiatives by the British Institute of Learning Disabilities designed to improve practice in relation to the use of reactive physical interventions with persons who display challenging behaviour. It follows on the publication of *Physical Interventions: A policy framework* (Harris et al, 1996) and the database, *Providers of Training on the Application of Physical Interventions* (BILD, 2000). A voluntary code of practice for trainers has also been produced as a first step towards establishing an accreditation mechanism for courses on physical management. The Code was sent out for consultation in July 2000 and was published by BILD in March 2001.

Contemporary approaches to challenging behaviour (LaVigna et al, 1989; Horner et al, 1990; Carr et al, 1990; Allen, 2000) suggest that successful interventions will involve two types of strategy.

First, behaviour change strategies will be required to help achieve short-term control over challenging behaviour and to develop adaptive, functionally equivalent or functionally alternative behaviours in the medium to long-term. Behaviour change strategies include ecological and antecedent change, skill development (self-help skills, functional communication, anger control etc.), and the use of differential reinforcement. Behaviour change strategies are proactive procedures and typically have to be maintained long-term.

Second, behaviour management strategies will be required to enable carers to respond to incidents of challenging behaviour when they occur. Behaviour management strategies include distraction and defusion techniques, self-protective (or 'breakaway') techniques, and minimal restraint. Behaviour management strategies are reactive procedures, and are generally designed for use in the short-term (although they too may be required in the long-term). In addition to making carers and service users safe, training in reactive strategies may be a critical element in maintaining community placements for people with learning disabilities and challenging behaviour (Allen, 1999; Green & Wray, 1999). They may also help facilitate the reduction of unnecessary anti-psychotic medication (Ahmed et al, 2000), and help set the conditions under which behaviour change strategies can be implemented (McDonald, 1997).

Several detailed and thorough analyses are available regarding the effectiveness of behaviour change strategies for persons with learning disabilities (Scotti et al, 1991; Carr et al, 1990; Didden, et al, 1997; Carr et al, 1999), and Harris (1996), who has reviewed the outcomes for the use of restraint as part of behavioural treatment. The need for evidence-based practice applies equally well to behaviour management strategies, and although a number of reviews on behaviour management in mental health are available (Fisher, 1994; Wing et al, 1998; Sailas

& Fenton, 1999), they have paid scant attention to the impact of training and excluded studies on persons with learning disabilities.

This is unfortunate, as persons with learning disabilities who challenge services are at high risk of experiencing physical interventions (Emerson, 1995; Sturmey, 1999). Furthermore, an evidence based approach to training in reactive strategies is important given the proliferation of behaviour management training approaches that currently exist. The BILD database, for example, lists over 70 providers of training within the United Kingdom; these trainers are delivering a bewildering array of different types of training to staff supporting persons with learning disabilities. In itself, this is clear evidence of the uncertainty that exists regarding the optimum training model for the carers of persons with learning disabilities and challenging behaviour.

Concerns have also been expressed about potential practical, ethical and legal issues regarding some forms of widely disseminated training (Hopton, 1995; Duff et al, 1996; Allen et al, 1997; Stirling & McHugh, 1998), while the dangers of providing inappropriate training were brutally exposed by a recent undercover documentary filmed within a social care home (MacIntyre, 1999).

The aim of this publication is to review the existing literature regarding training carers in behaviour management strategies. The review will assist trainers and commissioners in auditing outcomes of training programmes and provide evidence of the knowledge and skills which underpin staff competence in the workplace. Its intention is both to provide an academic review of the field and to provide useful practical information for training providers and training recipients. It has four principal objectives:

1.   To alert purchasers and providers to the types of outcomes that should be expected from behaviour management training.

2.   To identify future research needs in this area.

3.   To help shape up the process of training evaluation, and to assist trainers working in this field, by providing a range of sample measures of key dependent variables.

4.   To help inform the accreditation process referred to above by summarising the current knowledge on training outcomes.

II. Method

The review process commenced with an automated search of the following databases:

- Psychlit   1989–2000

- Medline   1966–2000

- Cochrane Data Base of Systematic Reviews   Issue 1, 2000

Search terms utilised included 'physical restraint', 'aggression', 'violence', 'training', 'learning disabilities', 'mental retardation', 'mental handicap', 'care staff', and 'education'.

As this search procedure yielded comparatively few relevant documents, a further manual search of potentially relevant papers and books was made. Additional reports were also provided by members of the British Institute of Learning Disability's Physical Intervention Trainer Group. Because of the shortage of published papers, research on all service users groups, rather than just those on learning disabilities, was included. The focus of the search was on manual (i.e. hands-on restraint by carers) rather than mechanical restraint (i.e. restraint via restrictive devices such as ties, belts and splints).

A total of 45 papers were finally identified for inclusion in the main body of the review. Three broad categories of papers were reviewed:

a. Quasi-experimental and Descriptive Quantitative

Only one published study featured the random allocation of subjects to experimental and control groups, and no studies achieved a true matching of control and experimental groups within between-group designs. The vast majority of studies were therefore quasi-experimental in nature. Although the quality of the research designs limits the confidence with which conclusions can be drawn, it was felt that a review of the available literature was still valuable as a benchmarking exercise.

The alternative, as a recent Cochrane review (Sailas & Fenton, 1999) of seclusion and restraint for serious mental illness found, is to set higher methodological inclusion criteria and to end up having no studies to review.

Three main types of quasi-experimental study were identified for the present review:

Within-subject control – a basic pre-post design in which a series of measures were given participants prior to the administration of training and then repeated following training. Any pre-post differences on the measures are attributed to the effects of the intervention.

Between-groups control – a control group design in which participants exposed to training are compared to participants who have not. Any between-group differences on study measures are attributed to the training intervention.

Descriptive quantitative studies – research typically involving simple pre-post comparisons on single variables (e.g. rates of injury) or post-training surveys.

b. Non-Quantitative Descriptive

These studies provided purely anecdotal, non-data driven accounts of training outcomes.

c. Unpublished Studies

Given the general low volume of published reports, a number of unpublished studies were also reviewed. These studies were mostly of a descriptive quantitative nature.

A small number of additional studies and reports were identified which, although they were not concerned with training in themselves, were relevant to reactive behaviour management training. A further 12 studies are included in this section.

For each of study types described above, summaries were provided concerning the study focus, measures and outcomes. The methods section makes reference to the sample size and reliability where available. Within the focus section, the specific training approach under study was specified where possible (given in italics), together with the nature of service user group supported, details of service setting and country of origin. The number of each study refers to its number within the reference list. Further details about the general principles of experimental design can be found in Breakwell et al (1995).

The summaries are provided in section III and an overview of the main results then follows in section IV.

III. Summary of Research Literature

a. Quasi-Experimental & Descriptive Quantitative Studies on Training Outcomes

The summary results for the quasi-experimental studies are shown in table 1 below.

Table 1: Quasi Experimental Studies

Study Number & Reference	Design	Focus	Measures	Outcomes
1. Allen et al	Descriptive, Time Series. N=7. Sample = long-stay residents within an acute admission unit. No reliability data.	*Positive Behaviour Management (Welsh Centre)*. Impact of training in a 6 bed residential treatment unit, adults with learning disabilities & challenging behaviour. UK	Frequency of behavioural incidents, use of restraint, as required medications, injuries to staff, injuries to service users.	Reductions in behaviour rate for most participants, trends in reduction of restraint, emergency medications; decommissioning of seclusion facility; significant reductions in staff & service user injuries.
4. Allen & Tynan	Between group & within subject. N=109. Cronbach's Alpha for scales used = .64 & .88.	*Positive Behaviour Management (Welsh Centre)*. Impact of training on staff supporting adults with learning disabilities & challenging behaviour in community services. UK	Aggression (Confidence Questionnaire), Reactive Strategies Questionnaire	Significant differences in both knowledge and confidence between trained and untrained groups, and also pre-post following administration of training to previously untrained staff.
6. Baker & Bissmire	Within subject, descriptive. N=17. Total sample of staff working in service. No reliability or validity measures.	*Strategies for Crisis Intervention and Prevention (SCIP)*. Impact of training in a 10 bed community residential service for people with learning disabilities & challenging behaviour. UK	Confidence questionnaire, perception of support offered by organisation, frequency of behavioural incidents, nature of staff responses.	Increase in confidence, increased tendency to use physical interventions, increased ratings of organisational support, no impact on overall rates of incidents.

Study Number & Reference	Design	Focus	Measures	Outcomes
7. Bell & Mollison	Within subject, descriptive. N=95. Total sample of individuals completing training. No reliability or validity measures.	*Therapeutic Crisis Intervention (TCI).* Impact of training on residential child care staff. UK	Knowledge questionnaire, evaluation questionnaires, semi-structured interviews	Pre-post improvements in knowledge that were essentially maintained at 6 month follow-up. Positive participant evaluation of workshops.
8. Bell & Stark	Within subject. N=14. Variety of reliability measures cited.	*TCI.* Development of standardised instrument to measure performance of restraint techniques. UK	Measures derived for evaluation of three specific physical interventions.	Inter-rater reliability of trainee performance significantly improved using instruments as compared to assessment based on expert opinion.
14. Carmel & Hunter	Descriptive. N=744. Total sample of staff in 27 wards. No reliability measures.	California Dept. Mental Health Training Programme. Forensic in-patient services. USA	Frequency of aggressive incidents, rates of staff injury.	Compliance with required standards in training for the management of aggression was associated with lower rates of staff injury but not with lower rates of assaultive behaviour.
30. Flannery et al	Descriptive. N=940. Total sample of staff in three facilities. No reliability measures.	*Assaulted Staff Action Programme.* Three mental health hospitals, nursing staff. USA	Rates of assaultive behaviour.	Significant reduction in rates of assaultive behaviour in last year quarter before programme introduced as compared to first quarter post training.
31. Forster et al	Descriptive. Analysis of records. No reliability measures.	Training in prevention of assaultive behaviour. 85 bed acute mental health facility. USA	Rates of seclusion, duration of seclusion/restraint, staff injuries.	14% reduction in restraint usage, 55% reduction in duration of seclusion/restraint episodes, 19% reduction in staff injuries.
33. Gertz	Descriptive. No details of methodology.	Impact of 2 day workshops in a mental health setting. USA	Frequency of incidents.	33% reduction in patient related accidents over two year period.

Study	Design/Sample	Measures	Results
35. Goodykoontz & Herrick	Within subject, Descriptive. N=27. Total sample of participants attending training programme. No reliability or validity measures.	Staff training in unit for persons with acute schizophrenia. USA	Burnout Scale, frequency of incidents, staff injuries.	No overall impact on burnout measures, reduction in aggressive incident frequency, anecdotal account of reduced injury.
44. Infantino & Musingo	Between group. N=96. Total sample of staff in direct care roles. No reliability measures.	*Aggression Control Techniques.* Mental health services. USA	Rates of assaultive behaviour, staff injuries, confidence	Trained staff significantly less likely to experience assaultive behaviour, non-significant trend suggesting less likely to be injured during assaultive incidents. 86% staff in receipt of training reported increased confidence.
46. Kalogjera et al	Descriptive. Analysis of 273 episodes of restraint & seclusion. No reliability measures.	Training in alternatives to restraint, communication skills. Adolescent psychiatric service. USA	Rates of seclusion, restraint, medication usage	64% reduction in seclusion & restraint episodes; no changes in medication usage.
48. Lehman et al	Within subject. N=144. 77% sample of all staff attending 8 workshops. No reliability measures.	Staff training programme in Veterans Hospital. USA	Knowledge of preventative techniques, self-confidence measure.	Significant improvements in knowledge and confidence post-training.
51. McDonnell	Within subject. N=21. Total sample of participants on course. Cronbach's Alpha for measures used .50, .92. Inter-rater reliability for video analysis = 94%.	*Studio III.* Primarily nursing staff supporting persons with learning disabilities. UK	Violent Incident Knowledge Test, Managing Challenging Behaviour Confidence Scale, and Restraint Role Play Test.	Significant pre-post differences in knowledge and confidence. All participants achieved high scores on the role play test.
53. McDonnell & Reeves	Descriptive. N= unknown. No reliability measures.	*Studio III* training introduced as part of a package of measures. Nursing staff supporting persons with learning disabilities and mental health problems. UK	Usage of seclusion and restraint.	Reduction in usage of both procedures post-training.

Study Number & Reference	Design	Focus	Measures	Outcomes
56. McGowan et al	Within subject. N=70. Sampling unclear. No reliability or validity measures.	Impact of training in three secure hospitals. Australia.	Staff confidence	Significant pre-post improvements.
58. Mortimer	Descriptive, Time Series. N=23, total population of staff on unit. No reliability measures.	Control & Restraint (C&R). 12 bed secure psychiatric ward. UK	Frequency, severity of behavioural incidents, targets of assault.	Major decrease in both number and severity of assaultive incidents over time; whereas patient-staff assaults decreased, patient-patient assaults increased.
60. Murray et al	Descriptive. N=50, not random sample. Inter-interviewer reliability 75–82% across items.	Social care staff supporting people with learning disabilities. UK	Confidence, experience of assaultive behaviour.	No differences between trained and untrained staff in experiencing aggression. Males who had received training reported feeling more confident.
62. Nunno et al	Within subject, Descriptive. N=104 for staff outcomes. Chronbach's Alpha for Confidence Scale= .69 & .52 (pre & post). No reliability data for indirect outcomes.	TCI. Residential child care facility, emotional and behaviour disorders. USA	Knowledge, confidence, frequency of incidents.	33% increase in knowledge score with some evidence of these scores being maintained at 9 month follow-up; significant changes on some confidence measures. Reduction in number of incidents and usage of restraint in one of four units studied.
63. Parkes	Descriptive. No reliability data.	C&R. 44 bed medium secure unit. UK	Nature of incidents, number of staff involved, perception of incidents.	Staff injuries increased overall post-training. Staff reported satisfaction with the techniques taught. No change in rates of injury to patients were observed, although some reported discomfort as a result of wrist-locks being applied. Staff resource requirements increased.

Study	Method / Reliability	Sample / Setting	Measures	Results
64. Paterson et al	Within subject. N=25. Total sample of participants on two courses. Test-retest reliability for questionnaires for 2/4 used = 74– 83%. Inter-rater reliability for role plays = .22 –1.00.	C&R. Nursing staff in mental health services. UK	Knowledge, General Health, Job satisfaction, Role Conflict Questionnaires. Role plays of de-escalation and physical intervention skills.	Significant changes in knowledge, stress, role conflict; improvements in all role play situations.
67. Phillips & Rudestam	Between group (with random allocation of subjects), within subject. Self-selecting sample. N=24. Inter-rater reliability for video analysis = .94 –.97.	Male staff in mental health. Comparison of effectiveness of didactic v. physical training in aggression management. USA	Hostility-Guilt Inventory, fear and aggression questionnaire, assessment of physical role play skill, post-training assault patterns.	Group receiving didactic and physical training produced superior ratings of physical competence , and lower ratings of fear and aggression as compared to groups that received didactic training only or no training controls. Similar results were obtained in terms of self-ratings. Physical competence was correlated with changes in fear and aggression scores. Follow-up measures indicated that the group receiving the combined training experienced fewer assaults and injuries.
69. Rice et al	Within subject, between groups, time series. N=125. Sampling unclear. Variety of reliability measures for both self-adminstered tests and observer measures.	Mental health staff from maximum security unit. Canada.	Four tests of theoretical and physical skills, self-report questionnaires on confidence etc., frequency of assaults	Significant improvements in physical skills, knowledge and personal effectiveness; latter endured at 6 week and 15 month follow-up. Decreases in number of incidents and injuries immediately post-training, but both then increased. Significant effect on working days lost due to injury.
71. Rosenthal et al	Descriptive. N=633. 23% response to postal survey. No reliability measures.	Nursing staff in general and mental health hospitals. USA	Nature of assaultive incidents, impact upon respondent.	Staff without training were three times more to encounter serious violence than staff that had training.

Study Number & Reference	Design	Focus	Measures	Outcomes
74. Smoot & Gonzales	Between group study of two units matched on size and function. N=35. No reliability measures.	Communication skills training. In-patient psychiatric unit staff. USA	Staff turnover & sickness, frequency of assaultive behaviour	Unit where training took place showed reductions in staff turnover, sickness, and restraint use, as compared to no training control. Control unit had bigger reduction in rates of assaultive behaviour.
75. SNMAC	Survey. Descriptive. N = 294.	C&R. Staff working in regional secure units and intensive care units in the UK	Length of training, injuries, time in post before training received	In last incident involving C&R, 19% staff, 11% service users were injured. 27% of respondents were injured during the training itself.
78. St.Thomas' Psychiatric Hospital	Descriptive. No reliability measures.	Mental Health Facility. Training in preventative & physical intervention skills. Canada	Rates of assaultive behaviour, injuries to staff and service users.	Year pre and post training compared. Rates of assaults decreased by 9.4%, staff injuries by 12% and client injuries 10.4%.
80. Thackray	Within subject, between group. N=236. Cronbach's Alpha =.92. for scale.	Therapeutics for Aggression. Community mental health centre, state hospital and state prison staff. USA	Confidence questionnaire.	Trained staff showed increases in confidence that essentially maintained at 18 month follow-up.
82. Van Den Pol et al	Multiple baseline, between group. N=13. S's demographic charac-teristics representative of total sample. Reliability for behavioural observations averaged above 90%	Range of self-protective procedures. Staff in large residential facility for persons with learning disability. USA	Performance of physical skills	Peer training effective in teaching and maintaining physical skills at 18 week follow-up. Social validity checks at 23 months follow-up demonstrated appropriate nature of skills taught.
84. Whittington et al	Descriptive. N=383. 38% response rate to postal questionnaires. No reliability measures.	General hospital staff. UK	Patterns and correlates of assaultive behaviour	Staff that had attended some form of violence training were more likely to be assaulted

b. Non-Quantitative Descriptive Reports on Training outcomes

The summary results for the non-data based descriptive studies are shown in table 2 below.

Table 2: Descriptive Reports

Study Number & Reference	Focus	Measures	Outcomes
18. Carton & Larkin	C&R. Impact of training on a single ward within a secure hospital. N=17. UK	Frequency, nature, targets of assaultive incidents.	Change in frequency of incidents as compared to an earlier study attributed to provision of training for whole staff team.
26. Edwards, R.	C&R. Nursing staff supporting persons with learning disability and challenging behaviour, intensive treatment service. N=11. UK	Semi-structured interviews. Perceptions of training impact.	Improved teamwork and co-ordination post-training.
27. Edwards, R.	C&R. Nursing staff supporting persons with learning disability and challenging behaviour, intensive treatment service. N=11. UK	Semi-structured interviews. Impact of gender on perceptions of training impact.	Female staff felt less dependent on male staff in managing aggressive incidents; males felt more able to let females intervene.
36. Green & Wray	Single case study. Breakaway training for parents of child with Prader Willi syndrome and challenging behaviour. UK	Carer confidence	Anecdotal account of improved confidence, community placement maintained.

Study Number & Reference	Focus	Measures	Outcomes
50. Martin	*Non-violent Crisis Intervention* (Crisis Prevention Institute) Nursing home staff supporting persons with dementia. USA	Use of role play to test competence in physical interventions.	Described as an effective means of staff training.
81. Titus	*TCI*. Residential child services. USA	Rates of restraint usage, duration of restraint, injuries to staff.	Restraint usage decreased but duration increased. Rates of injuries increased.

c. *Unpublished Reports on Training Outcomes*

The summary results for the unpublished studies are shown in table 3 below.

Table 3: Unpublished Studies

Study Number & Reference	Design	Focus	Measures	Outcomes
13. Brookes	Descriptive, time series. N and sampling unclear. No reliability measures.	*C&R*. Prison Service. UK	Rates of assault, sick leave, confidence.	Pre-post reduction in rates of assaults, sick leave; incremental increase in confidence over duration of two week course.
19. Chadwick	Descriptive. N=43. Sample of all children experiencing restraint over study period. No reliability measures.	*TCI & C&R*. Residential child care. UK	Pattern of usage of techniques, injuries.	Higher rates of injury to staff than children. Techniques generally viewed favourably by staff.

Study	Design	Setting	Measures	Findings
22. Crossley & Burns	Descriptive. Five community houses. No reliability measures.	Positive Behaviour Management (Welsh Centre). Community residential care supporting persons with learning disabilities. UK	Frequency, nature of incidents, injuries.	Some evidence of reduction in incidents, injuries; anecdotal reports of increased confidence.
32. Gallon & McDonnell	Descriptive. Total sample of staff on series of training courses. N=29	Studio III. Mental health, elderly mentally infirm. Impact of training on staff previously trained in C&R. UK	Confidence ratings, acceptability of techniques.	72% respondents felt that the techniques devised for use with persons with learning disabilities were applicable to the other user groups, 79% felt that they offered an alternative to C&R. Significant pre-post improvements in confidence across 6 courses. Higher scores for males both pre and post.
40. Heron	Descriptive. N=23. Sampling unclear. No reliability measures.	TCI. Residential child care. UK	Retention of knowledge and techniques; confidence in techniques.	Retention of theory poor. Almost 40% of staff were not confident about their ability to implement physical techniques. Some techniques were considered ineffective/dangerous.
45. Judd	Descriptive. N=28. Postal survey, response rate unknown. No reliability measures.	C&R. Mental health, nursing staff. UK	Course feedback, impact on service, user.	Anecdotal reports of increased confidence.
52. McDonnell & Jones	Within subject. N=275. Total sample of participants in 15 training courses. Cronbach's Alpha for Confidence Scale = .92.	Studio III. Community staff supporting persons with learning disabilities. UK	As in study 51.	Replicated results of earlier study.

Study Number & Reference	Design	Focus	Measures	Outcomes
57. Miles	Descriptive. N=17, sample = 50% response to postal survey. No reliability measures.	*Positive Behaviour Management (Welsh Centre).* Social care staff supporting persons with learning disabilities. UK	Experience of aggression, satisfaction with training, physical interventions.	Anecdotal reports of increased confidence, low rates of usage of taught interventions.
61. Nethell	Descriptive. N=29, 67% response rate to postal questionnaire sent to individual representative (not defined) of staff in receipt of training. No reliability measures.	*Positive Behaviour Management (Welsh Centre).* Health & social care staff supporting persons with learning disabilities. UK	Effectiveness, ease of application of interventions, confidence.	Some evidence of increased confidence, carers able to implement taught moves most of time but difficulties in implementing also common. Failure to access follow-up training a common problem.

d. Reports on Other Aspects of Physical Interventions

The studies cited below are not concerned with training outcomes per se but are of relevance to reactive training.

Study Number & Reference	Design	Focus	Measures	Outcomes
2. Allen	Between-group. Sampling according to specific criteria relating to user status. N=47. Variety of reliability measures reported.	Factors predicting community placement breakdown of persons with learning disabilities. UK. Training model in place *Positive Behaviour Management (Welsh Centre)*	Series of personal and organisational variables.	Failure to provide training in reactive strategies identified as a risk factor for break down.

Study	Sample/Method	Setting	Focus	Findings
5. Ahmed et al	Between-group. N= 56. Sample selected by consultant psychiatrist referral. Variety of reliability measures reported.	Reduction in anti-psychotic medication in persons with learning disabilities. UK	Impact on challenging behaviour & adaptive behaviour.	Presence of policy on reactive strategies, staff training in reactive strategies predicted the ability to successfully reduce medication.
21. Corrigan et al	Multiple Baseline. N=22. Sampling procedure unclear. No reliability measures.	Mental health facility. Impact of a series of initiatives to improve proactive programming. USA	Rates of aggression & restraint use.	27% reduction in aggressive incidents for staff skills training programme plus token economy, 41% reduction in restraint use with token economy
24. Duff & Gray	C&R. Analysis of 91 incidents of violence.	Four hospital wards where C&R use was approved for use. UK	Correlates of C&R use.	Males & persons with schizophrenia were more likely to experience C&R.
41. Hill & Spreat	Descriptive. N=284. No reliability measures.	Institutional residential facility for persons with learning disabilities. USA	Staff injury rates.	Injury rates for both personal and mechanical restraint were higher for emergency, unplanned restraint interventions than for planned interventions.
54. McDonnell & Sturmey	Within subject, between groups. N=88. No reliability measures, although measurement tool is reported to be well validated in previous studies.	Studio III. Educational and residential care staff supporting persons with learning disabilities. UK	Comparison of three different types of restraint method via Treatment Evaluation Inventory	Chair restraint produced superior social validity ratings compared to floor restraint.
55. McDonnell et al	Within subject. N=60. Sampling procedure unclear. No reliability measures.	Studio III. University students. UK	Comparison of three different types of restraint method via Treatment Evaluation Inventory	Chair restraint produced superior social validity ratings compared to floor restraint.

Study Number & Reference	Design	Focus	Measures	Outcomes
59. Murphy et al	Survey. N = 26. Variety of reliability & validity measures reported.	Residential treatment unit for persons with learning disabled offenders. UK	Follow-up study on users' views on care at the unit & current quality of life	63% of those who remembered being restrained felt angry about the event, 25% felt sad or scared. No individual felt positive about the experience of being restrained.
68. Rangecroft et al	Descriptive. Examination of all incidents occurring over a six-month period. No reliability measures.	Institution for persons with learning disabilities. Impact of new monitoring procedures. UK	Rates of intra-muscular emergency medication use, restraint use.	Significant changes towards the use of oral emergency medication (33% increase) and away from intra-muscular, 29% reduction in rate restraint.
76. Spreat et al	Descriptive. N=231. Total adult population of facility. 98% reliability for data abstracted from records between researchers.	Institutional residential facility for persons with learning disabilities. USA	Client injury rates.	Risk of injury was highest with unplanned, personal restraints. Planned, mechanical restraint had the lowest injury rates. Emergency mechanical restraint was applied for the longest duration.
79. Sturmey	Descriptive. N=300. Sampling procedure unclear – total population? No reliability measures.	Institutional residential facility for persons with learning disabilities. USA	Rates and correlates of restraint use.	11% of sample had experienced relatively brief restraint, 4% more prolonged daily restraint. The presence of externally directed behaviours correlated with restraint use.

IV. Summary of Key Findings

This section provides an overview of the research results according to the main dependent variables studied. The material is divided into three sub-sections dealing with the nature of the client groups and techniques studied, the direct effects and the indirect effects of training. Direct training effects are concerned with the immediate effects of training, and relate primarily to the impact of training on participants (e.g. confidence levels, knowledge levels etc.). Indirect effects are secondary consequences of the training, and relate mainly to the impact of the training in the work place (e.g. impact on the number of aggressive incidents experienced, reactive management practices etc.). For each type of training outcome, both positive and negative research findings will be identified. The numbers in parentheses refer to the study number in the reference list.

1. Characteristics of the Service User Groups

The number of studies devoted to specific service user groups are shown in the following table:

Table 4: Studies by Service User Groups

Service User Group	Quasi-experimental	Descriptive Reports	Unpublished Reports	Other	Total
Learning Disabilities	7	3	2	10	22
Mental Health	18	1	4	2	25
Child Services	3	1	2	0	6
Other	2	1	1	0	4

Learning disabilities and mental health were by far the most commonly researched populations overall, making up 39% and 44% of the total number of studies reviewed respectively. Mental health services formed the focus of the majority of quasi-experimental studies (60%) however. Most of the overall studies reviewed (58%) originated in the United Kingdom; a further 37% came from the United States.

2. Characteristics of the Training Techniques

A breakdown of the specific training approaches studied in the literature is provided in table 5 below:

Table 5: Percentage of studies featuring specific training approaches

Training Programme	Quasi-experimental studies (%)	Descriptive Reports (%)	Unpublished Reports (%)	Other (%)	Total (%)
Crisis Prevention Institute	0	16.6	0	0	1.9
Control & Restraint	13	50	30	20	21.6
Positive Behaviour Management (Welsh Centre)	7	0	30	20	11.7
Strategies for Crisis Intervention & Prevention	3	0	0	0	1.9
Studio III	7	0	20	40	11.7
Therapeutics for Aggression	3	0	0	0	1.9
Therapeutic Crisis Intervention	10	16.6	20		11.7
Not known	57	16.6	0	20	37.3

Control & Restraint was the most commonly studied approach overall. This is somewhat misleading however in that C&R has become a generic term that encompasses a number of different approaches (Wright, 1999; SNMAC, 1999). It cannot therefore be assumed that the studies identified as researching the impact of this approach were actually studying the same thing.

Almost 38% of papers overall reported on methods of intervention that either utilised idiosyncratic training packages or packages that were not identifiable from the information given; this figure rose to 57% for quasi-experimental studies. This has obvious implications for the interpretation and replication of the studies in question.

As regards the approaches that were designed specifically for the use with carers supporting persons with learning disability, 46% of overall papers concerned the Studio III model, 46% Positive Behaviour Management (Welsh Centre) and 8% SCIP.

3. Direct Measures of Training Outcome

The findings reported in this section and the one that follows provide a basic summary of the results reported in the research literature on reactive behaviour management. At this stage, and for reasons that will be stated in the discussion, these results must be regarded as very preliminary findings and treated with caution. Additional research is required before these outcomes can be viewed with more certainty. The numbers in parentheses refer to the study number in the reference list.

a. Participant Knowledge
Positive:
- Trained staff are more knowledgeable than untrained staff (4)

- Pre-post training measures show an increase in knowledge (4, 6, 48, 51, 62, 64, 69)

- Gains in knowledge can be maintained at 6 months follow-up (7)

- Trained staff may be more able to identify the precursors of aggressive incidents and to identify appropriate interventions (48)

Negative:
- Retention of theoretical knowledge may be poor (40)

b. Participant Confidence
Positive:
- Trained staff are more confident than untrained staff (4, 44, 60, 80)

- Pre-post training measures show an increase in confidence (4, 6, 32, 48, 51, 52, 56, 62)

- Differences in confidence levels may still be maintained at 18 months follow-up (80)

- Confidence increases incrementally over the duration of a training course (13)

- This confidence may endure after trainees have experienced actual aggressive incidents post-training (48)

- Female staff may feel less dependent on males for support in managing aggression post-training (27)

- Burnout ratings may decrease post-training (35)

Negative:
- Impact on confidence may be low (40)

- There may be a gender effect for training, with female staff experiencing little or no improvement in confidence (32, 40, 60)

c. Participant Competence in physical interventions:
Positive:
- Trainees can successfully master a range of physical interventions (51, 52, 64, 69)

- Role play may play an important part in skill development (51, 82)

- Trainees general respond positively to role play (7)

- Standardised approaches to assessing physical competence can produce high rates of inter-observer agreement (8, 51, 69)

- Peer tutoring systems can be an effective means of teaching physical skills (82)

- Changes in physical competence may be positively correlated with changes in levels of fear and aggression (67)

- The number of techniques taught should be minimised to enhance retention and reduce confusion (8)

- Skill retention is likely to be enhanced when trainees are taught to saturation point (8)

Negative:
- Role play can be viewed as repetitive if over-used (7)

- Role play can generate high levels of emotion and anxiety and participants need to be properly de-briefed (7)

- Older participants may respond less favourably to role play (51)

- Rates of inter-rater agreement in the assessment of physical skills may be very poor (8)

- Staff may 'freeze' during attacks & not apply the procedures taught (63)

- Trainees with poorer physical skills are likely to demonstrate more aggressive behaviour in role plays (67)

- Staff may have little confidence in taught techniques (40)

Based on the results of studies into the effectiveness of CPR (cardio-pulmonary resuscitation) training, Bell & Stark (1998) have suggested that the acquisition and retention of physical intervention skills may be improved by training only one technique at a time, allowing adequate time to practice moves and teaching techniques to saturation point, building in regular refresher training, and systematically assessing the competence of participants.

4. Indirect Measures of Training Outcome

a. Rates of challenging behaviour

Positive:

- Rates of behavioural incidents may decline post-training (1, 18, 30, 35, 58, 62)

- Severity of behavioural incidents may decline post-training (58)

- Trained staff may be less likely to experience assaultive behaviour (71)

- Improving training & support for behaviour change strategies can reduce rates of aggressive behaviour (21)

Negative:

- Rates of behavioural incidents may not change post-training (6, 48, 62)

- Decreases in rates of assaultive behaviour may not maintain (69)

- Trained staff may experience higher rates of assaultive behaviour (but this may reflect the fact that their increased skill results in them being asked to manage more aggressive situations) (84)

- While assaults between service user and staff may decrease, assaults between service users may increase post-training (58)

b. Rates of use of reactive strategies

Positive:

- The use of restraint may decline post-training (1, 23, 31, 46, 53, 74, 81)

- The use of as required medications may decline over time (1, 23)

- The need for seclusion may reduce (1, 23, 31, 46, 53, 74)

- The duration of restraint and seclusion may decrease (31)

- Improving training & support for behaviour change strategies can reduce rates of restraint use (21)

Negative:

- Rates of use of physical interventions may increase (6)

- Duration of restraints may increase (81)

c. Injury rates

Positive:

- Injuries to carers may decline post-training (1, 14, 31, 33, 44, 78)

- Injuries to service users may decline post-training (1, 78)

- Planned physical interventions carry less risk of injury to carers and service users than unplanned interventions (41, 76)

Negative:
- Injuries to carers may remain unchanged or increase post-training (23, 63, 81)

- Service users may express discomfort with certain techniques (63)

- Certain techniques may be associated with higher risk of service user injury or fatality (25, 34, 40, 65, 66, 75)

- Certain techniques appear to pose quite considerable risks to staff during the training period itself (75)

- Staff may be injured whilst applying techniques in practice (41, 75, 76)

- Service users may continue to report negative feelings about experiencing restraint a considerable time afterwards (59)

5. Wider Findings
Positive:
- Seated restraint appears more socially acceptable than floor restraint (54, 55)

- Staff retention and sickness may be reduced by training (74)

- Training may generate very positive participant and management feedback (52, 69, 74)

- Improving proactive interventions can reduce rates of aggressive behaviour and the use of physical interventions (21)

- Rates of use of restraint and intra-muscular as required medication may be reduced by improved monitoring (23, 68)

- Reactive behaviour management may be an important variable in avoiding placement breakdown (2, 36)

- The development of clear policies in restraint use and the provision of restraint use may help reduce unnecessary anti-psychotic medication usage (5)

Negative:

- In the absence of a co-ordinated organisational response (in terms of policy & guidelines), training impact is reduced (7, 62)

- Newly appointed staff may have to wait a considerable time before receiving training (44, 75).

- Refresher training may be provided infrequently (61, 81)

- The impact of training may be reduced by having insufficient staff resources to implement techniques and by high rates of staff turnover (81)

- Only one study has sought the views of persons with learning disabilities about being subject to restraint (59)

Discussion

The existing research literature suggests that training carers in behaviour management skills may produce a variety of positive direct and indirect benefits. Staff that receive training appear to be more knowledgeable about appropriate behaviour management practices. They are also likely to feel more confident (although this effect may be less significant for female staff), and can be effectively taught physical intervention skills. In the workplace, staff training may decrease rates of challenging behaviour and the use of reactive strategies. Injuries to both carers and service users may also be reduced. Unfortunately, the research indicates that none of the above outcomes can be guaranteed from training, and negative results have also been observed in each of the above areas.

At this stage, these findings need to be viewed as being preliminary statements as the overall volume of evidence concerning the outcomes of behaviour management training is comparatively small. Given that virtually all the identified studies were at best quasi-experimental in nature, and that measures of reliability and validity were often not provided, the overall strength of the evidence available in support of the outcomes quoted can only be described as weak. This conclusion is in accordance with previous more general reviews of research into the management of violence (Royal College of Psychiatrists, 1998).

The tension created by the difficulty of applying robust research designs to this topic and the need for evidence-based practice has been well described by Sailas & Fenton. In their review of seclusion and restraint use in severe mental illness they concluded that:

> *'The reviewers acknowledge the very great difficulty of carrying out controlled trials in people with challenging behaviours. Nevertheless, the complete lack of trial-derived evidence is surprising given the invasiveness of seclusion and restraint and its continued use over time. This dearth may*

highlight a belief that they are such effective, satisfactory, interventions that there is not the need for evaluation in randomised trials. . . . Randomising different techniques of seclusion or restraint, or comparing the former to alternatives, may be thought to be controversial. Conversely, continuing to use a poorly investigated set of 'invasive' treatments on very significant numbers of people may seem equally questionable'

Sailas & Fenton (1999) p. 9

The message here is very clear. While achieving adequate scientific control may be problematic in relation to studies on behaviour management, the intrusiveness of the techniques under study, and the potential risks associated with them, demands a higher quality evidence base than that which is currently available. As stated in the introduction, the need for evidence-based practice in relation to behaviour management is no different than is the case with behaviour change strategies; in some ways, this need is even greater.

In addition to their methodological inadequacies, comparatively few existing studies refer to clearly identifiable training approaches. Even when positive results are cited, the key independent training variables responsible for these outcomes cannot therefore be identified. Similarly, the methods of instruction utilised are often not clearly described. It is therefore impossible to ascertain the extent to which differences in training methods (rather than in the material taught) may explain differences in training outcomes. Training duration may also vary greatly, even within different courses employing the same training reactive training approach (SNMAC, 1999).

No comparative studies of different training approaches exist, and for this reason it is not possible to reach any conclusions about preferred training approaches for use with persons with learning disabilities. This is something more than an academic issue. As indicated earlier, certain types of physical interventions appear to cause a degree of pain or discomfort to service users.

Concern over this issue has been raised by a number of authorities. In 1995, for example, the Royal College of Psychiatrists reported that:

'There must be grave concern that the widespread and deliberate use of pain, whether actual or threatened, has become part of the management of patients without consideration as to the moral and ethical issues involved. There is no evidence in the literature that the use of pain in Control and Restraint has been examined to determine its relevance. Its role becomes particularly problematic and hazardous where the patient's perception of pain is altered (as might occur with learning disability, autism or various psychiatric states).'

RCP (1995) p. 6

Biersdorff (1991, 1994) has provided some evidence that some persons with learning disabilities may indeed experience heightened pain thresholds. The implication of this finding is that an excessive degree of force may be required to elicit a response to painful stimuli within this population.

It is therefore of interest to note that much of the available research on reactive behaviour management in learning disabilities has involved physical intervention techniques that have avoided pain-compliance procedures. Between them, the studies concerned have demonstrated all the major positive outcomes identified in the review without having to inflict pain. Given the small data base and design weaknesses already described, the possibility that pain-compliance methods may not be required in learning disability should be viewed as an encouraging possibility rather than as a definitive conclusion.

An additional technique-related concern is that certain holds (notably prone restraint and 'basket' holds) appear to be associated with increased risk of positional asphyxia (Paterson, 1998; General Accounting Office, 1999). Positional asphyxia occurs when a person's body position interferes with their respiration, and death from asphyxia or suffocation results as a consequence. While the research into the relationship between restraint position and increased cardio-vascular distress has produced equivocal results to date (Chan et al, 1997; Roggla et al, 1997), this research has been conducted on healthy volunteers. Persons with learning disabilities are known to be at increased risk for a whole host of health problems (Welsh Office, 1992) and some of these problems may in turn increase their susceptibility to positional asphyxia. The results of research on healthy subjects may therefore not have much relevance to this population. This is a critical area for future research.

The interpretation of indirect training outcomes poses particular problems as a wide range of variables other than the training itself may affect rates of aggressive behaviour, reactive strategy use etc. An earlier review of quantitative studies into seclusion (Gutheil, 1984) suggested that the frequency of usage of both seclusion and physical interventions would escalate as a consequence of increases in:

- levels of violent behaviour in the target population

- the proportion of involuntary patients and perpetrators of violent crime

- legal, political, professional and economic attacks on the service system

- inter-staff tensions and disagreements

- the undermining of on-site decisions.

And by decreases in:

- number of staff

- number of senior, experienced staff

- number of male staff

- availability of public support for the service

- staff morale & sense of security

- available alternatives

The provision of training in physical interventions is therefore only one of many complex variables that may impact on measures of reactive training. This has implications both for organisation-wide interventions and research design.

A further complication in assessing indirect training outcomes is the inadequate collection of baseline data prior to the introduction of training initiatives. It is well known that aggressive incidents (and therefore the procedures adopted for managing aggressive incidents) are often under reported. Rates of aggressive behaviour and physical interventions may therefore appear to increase post-training simply because recording practices improve as a result of the training programme.

V. Conclusions: Towards Evidence Based Practice

Two main sets of general conclusions can be drawn from the present review. The first relates to the need to improve the quality of our knowledge base concerning reactive behaviour management training. The second concerns implications that can be drawn from the present research about improving the routine measurement of training outcomes.

1. *Implications for Future Research*

The review identified a number of problems with existing research. These related principally to the inadequacy of the design of studies and a lack of detail about procedures and teaching methods employed. Each area will be discussed in turn and recommendations for improving practice suggested.

a. Improving research design

In general, the research in this field needs to:

- Expand the research database on behaviour management in general and in learning disability in particular

- Produce better controlled studies that allow firmer conclusions to be drawn

- Routinely include measures of reliability and validity

- Conduct research that features multiple outcomes on both direct and indirect training effects

- Conduct research that obtains the views of service users

b. Specifying training content

As stated in the earlier discussion, evaluating the outcomes of training is difficult when the content of the training is largely unknown. No core syllabus exists for training in behaviour management, but Wright's (1999) review of the literature suggests that training should contain the following ingredients:

- Principles and practice of verbal de-escalation skills

- Introductory material on the legal and ethical aspects of the use of force in behaviour management

- An emphasis on protecting the dignity of the service user

- An identification of the potential risk factors that may be implicated in restraint procedures (e.g., positional asphyxia, agitated delirium, atlanto-axial instability)

- A range of physical interventions including breakaway techniques, techniques for moving service users, and restraint

- Post-incident care for both staff and service users

The Health & Safety Commission (1997) have also suggested that incident reporting systems should be included in training courses.

Future research needs to ensure that sufficient detail is provided concerning the content of what was actually taught on courses in order to enable firm conclusions to be drawn and replications to be conducted. The above headings provide a possible standardised menu via which such descriptions could be made. In addition, the anticipated links between training content and improved staff performance in the workplace need to be made explicit.

c. Specifying Teaching Methods

The methods used to teach participants also need to be more clearly specified within research studies. Key variables will include:

- The duration of training

- Trainer: trainee ratios

- The amount of theoretical teaching

- The amount of physical practice

- The balance between preventative material and reactive material

- The number of physical interventions taught

- Whether or not use of role-play was used

- The availability of follow-up training.

Future studies must give exact descriptions of how the training being studied was provided. The above list represents the minimum requirements for such a description.

d. Specific Research Issues

A number of clear research issues emerge from the review. These include the need:

- To conduct comparative studies into the effectiveness of different training programmes and their ability to meet clearly defined occupational standards in behaviour management

- To conduct comparative studies into the effectiveness of different teaching strategies and their ability to meet clearly defined occupational standards in behaviour management

- To conduct comparative studies into the social validity of different training programmes for carers of persons with learning disabilities

- To conduct detailed bio-mechanical and physiological assessments of the risks involved in specific techniques (most particularly with respect to any procedures thought to be implicated in positional asphyxia)

- To ascertain whether increased knowledge and confidence translates into better working practices in the workplace and the precise nature of the relationship between these variables

- To conduct studies which conduct follow-up measures of training outcomes in order to assess whether initial training gains are maintained in the work place

- To ascertain when decay in confidence and physical competence may occur in order to provide more specific guidance about the timing of refresher training

- To assess the extent to which trainer:trainee ratios impacts on outcome measures

- To assess the relative contribution of different training elements' (e.g. theory vs. physical skills practice) impact on confidence and performance

- To investigate the extent to which increased carer confidence may set the scene for the implementation of positive behavioural interventions

- To research the mechanisms which may have a differential effect on confidence levels in males and females and how this differential impact may be overcome.

In order to fulfil this research agenda, it will be necessary to develop a range of instruments for measuring training outcomes that can be applied across a range of different training models. In the bulk of the work carried out to date, idiosyncratic measures related to the specific type of training being evaluated have typically been employed. The development of reliable and valid measures that can be generalised across different behaviour management training programmes is therefore a research task in itself.

2. Implications for the Routine Measurement of Training Outcomes

The research literature suggests that the following are viable and appropriate minimum outcome measures that should be collected by trainers during initial training courses for staff:

- A pre and post assessment as to whether participants' knowledge of behaviour management principles has improved as a result of the training; this assessment should focus on both the preventative and reactive elements of training

- A pre and post assessment of participant confidence

- General feedback on the quality of the training provided

- An assessment of competence in the performance of physical management skills.

For refresher training sessions, repetition of the confidence and physical competence measures would be desirable. Some example measures and guidance for assessing physical skills are provided in the appendix.

Commissioners of training should aim to measure the following indirect outcomes of training:

- Rates of behavioural incidents pre and post training

- Rates of use of all alternative reactive procedures (and not just physical interventions) pre and post training. This will enable collateral changes in non-physical procedures to be assessed.

- Rates of injuries to both service users and staff.

Examples of analyses of indirect training outcomes are also provided in the appendix. In addition to these outcomes, commissioners should closely monitor rates of attendance at training and refresher training.

References

1. Allen, D., McDonald, L., Dunn, C. & Doyle, T. (1987) Changing care staff approaches to the management of aggressive behaviour in a residential treatment unit for persons with mental retardation and challenging behaviour. *Research in Developmental Disabilities*, **18**, 101–112.

2. Allen, D. (1999) Success and failure in community placements for people with learning disabilities and challenging behaviour: An analysis of key variables. *Journal of Mental Health*, **8**, 3, 307–320.

3. Allen, D. (2000) Recent research on physical aggression in persons with intellectual disability: An overview. *Journal of Intellectual & Developmental Disability*, **25**, 1, 41–57.

4. Allen, D. & Tynan, H. (2000) Responding to aggressive behaviour: The impact of training on staff knowledge and confidence. *Mental Retardation*, **38**, 2, 97–104.

5. Ahmed, Z., Fraser, W., Kerr, M.P., Kiernan, C., Emerson, E., Robertson, J., Felce, D., Allen, D., Baxter, H. & Thomas, J. (2000) Reducing antipsychotic medication in people with a learning disability. *British Journal of Psychiatry*, **176**, 42–46.

6. Baker, P.A. & Bissimire, D. (2000) A pilot study on the use of physical intervention in crisis management of people with intellectual disabilities who present challenging behaviour. *Journal of Applied Research in Intellectual Disabilities*, 13, 38–45.

7. Bell, L. & Mollison, A. (1995) *An evaluation of Therapeutic Crisis Intervention Training in Grampian Region*. Stirling: University of Stirling.

8. Bell, L. & Stark, C. (1998) *Measuring competence in physical restraint skills in residential child care*. Edinburgh: Scottish Office Central Research Unit.

9. Biersdorff, K.K. (1991) Pain insensitivity and indifference. Alternative explanations for some medical catastrophes. *Mental Retardation*, **29**, 359–362.

10. Biersdorff, K.K. (1994) Incidence of significantly altered pain experience among individuals with developmental disability. *American Journal on Mental Retardation*, **98**, 5, 619–631.

11. Breakwell, G.M., Hammond, S., & Fife-Shaw, C. (1995) *Research Methods in Psychology*. London: Sage.

12. British Institute of Learning Disabilities (2000) Providers of Training on the Application of Physical Interventions. Kidderminster: BILD.

13. Brookes, M. (1988) *Control and Restraint Techniques. A study into its effectiveness at HMP Gartree*. London: Home Office, Prison Department.

14. Carmel, H. & Hunter, M. (1990) Compliance with training in managing assaultive behaviour and injuries from inpatient violence. *Hospital and Community Psychiatry*, **41**, 5, 558–560.

15. Carr, E.G., Robinson, S. & Palumbo, L.W. (1990) The wrong issue: Aversive vs. nonaversive treatment. The right issue: functional vs. nonfunctional treatment. In Repp, A. & Singh, N.N. (Eds.) *Perspectives on the Use of Nonaversive and Aversive Interventions for Persons with Developmental Disabilities* (pp. 361–379). Sycamore, Il: Sycamore Publishing Company.

16. Carr, E.G., Robinson, S., Taylor, J.C. & Carlson, J.I. (1990) *Positive approaches to the treatment of severe behaviour problems in persons with developmental disabilities: A review and analysis of reinforcement and stimulus-based procedures.* Monograph of the Association for Persons with Severe Handicaps No. 4. Seattle: The Association for Persons with Severe Handicaps.

17. Carr, E.G., Horner, R.H., Turnbull, A.P. , Marquis, J.G., McLaughlin, D.M., McAtee, M.L., Smith, C.E., Ryan, K.A., Ruef, M.B., & Doolabh, A. (1999) *Positive Behavioural Support for People with Developmental Disabilities: A Research Synthesis*. Washington: American Association on Mental Retardation.

18. Carton, G. & Larkin, E. (1991) Reducing violence in a special hospital. *Nursing Standard*, **5**, 17, 29–31.

19. Chadwick, J. (1995) *Restraint monitoring August 1994 to 28 February 1995 Children & families Services-Community Services Devon*. Exeter: Devon Social services.

20. Chan, T.C., Vilke, G.M., Neuman, T. & Clausen, J.L. (1997) Restraint position and positional asphyxia. *Annals of Emergency Medicine*, **30**, 578–586.

21. Corrigan, P.E., Holmes, D.L., Basit, A., Delaney, E., Gleason, W., Buican, B. & McCracken, S. (1995) The effects of interactive staff training on staff programming and patient aggression in a psychiatric inpatient ward. *Behavioural Interventions*, **10**, 1, 17–32.

22. Crossley, R. & Burns, J. (1999) *Responding to Aggression & Violence. The effectiveness of theoretical and practical training April- June 1997/ April-June 1998*. Manchester: BHRV.

23. Davidson, N.A., Hemingway, M.J. & Wysocki, T. (1984) Reducing the use of restrictive procedures in a residential facility. *Hospital and Community Psychiatry*, **35**, 2, 164–167.

24. Duff, L., Gray, R. & Bristow, F. (1996) The use of control and restraint in acute psychiatric units. *Psychiatric Care*, **3**, 6, 230–234.

25. Edwards, R. (undated) *A Safety Audit on Brodie Youth Care Centre*. Central Regional Council

26. Edwards, R. (1999) The laying on of hands: nursing staff talk about physical restraint. *Journal of Learning Disabilities for Nursing, Health and Social Care*, **3**, 3, 136–143.

27. Edwards, R. (1999) Physical restraint and gender: Whose role it is anyway? *Learning Disability Practice*, **2**, 3, 12–15.

28. Emerson, E. (1995) *Challenging Behaviour. Analysis and intervention in people with learning difficulties*. Cambridge: Cambridge University Press.

29. Fisher, W.A. (1994) Restraint and Seclusion: A Review of the Literature. *American Journal of Psychiatry*, **151**, 11, 1584–1591.

30. Flannery, R.B., Hanson, M.A., Penk, W.E., Goldfinger, S., Pasta, G.J. & Navon, M.A. (1998) Replicated declines in assault rates after implementation of the Assaulted Staff Action Program. *Psychiatric Services*, **49**, 241–243.

31. Forster, P.L., Cavness, C. & Phelps, M.A. (1999) Staff training decreases use of seclusion and restraint in an acute psychiatric hospital. *Archives of Psychiatric Nursing*, **8**, 5, 269–271.

32. Gallon, I. & McDonnell, A. (2000) *The development and evaluation of a staff training package in non-aversive behaviour management: An alternative to control and restraint?* Bath: Studio III Training Systems.

33. Gertz, B. (1980) Training for prevention of assaultive behaviour in a psychiatric setting. *Hospital & Community Psychiatry*, **31**, 9, 628–630.

34. General Accounting Office (1999) *Mental Health: Improper Restraint or Seclusion Use Places People at Risk*. Washington:GAO.

35. Goodykoontz, L. & Herrick, C.A. (1990) Evaluation of an inservice education program regarding aggressive behaviour on a psychiatric unit. *Journal of Continuing Education in Nursing*, **21**, 3, 129–133.

36. Green, T. & Wray, J. (1999) Enabling carers to access specialist training in breakaway techniques: a case study. *Journal of Learning Disabilities for Nursing, Health & Social Care*, **3**, 1, 34–38.

37. Guthiel, T.G. (1984) Review of individual quantitative studies. In Tardiff, K. (Ed.) *The Psychiatric Uses of Seclusion and Restraint*. Washington: American Psychiatric Press.

38. Harris, J. (1996) Physical restraint procedures for managing challenging behaviours presented by mentally retarded adults and children. *Research in Developmental Disabilities*, **17**, 2, 99–134.

39. Harris, J., Allen, D., Comick, M., Jefferson, A. & Mills, R. (1996) Physical Interventions: A Policy Framework. Kidderminster: BILD.

40. Heron, G. (1996) *An analysis of the effectiveness of Therapeutic Crisis Intervention within social work residential child care*. Postgraduate Diploma Thesis: Jordan Hill College.

41. Hill, J. & Spreat, S. (1987) Staff injury rates associated with the implementation of contingent restraint. *Mental Retardation*, **25**, 3, 141–145.

42. Hopton, J. (1995) Control and restraint in contemporary psychiatric nursing: some ethical considerations. *Journal of Advanced Nursing*, **22**, 110–115.

43. Horner, R.H., Dunlap, G., Koegel, R.L., Carr, E.G., Sailor, W., Anderson, J., Albin, R.W. & O'Neil, R.E. (1990) Towards a technology of "nonaversive" behavioural support. *Journal of the Association for Persons with Severe Handicaps*, 15, 125–132.

44. Infantino, J.A. & Musingo, S. (1985) Assaults and injuries among staff with and without training in aggression control techniques. *Hospital and Community Psychiatry*, 36, 12, 1312–1314.

45. Judd, M. (1996) *Control & Restraint Training: Retrospective survey of nurses*. London: Clinical Audit Department, Camden & Islington Community Health Services NHS Trust.

46. Kalogjera, I.L., Bedi, A., Watson, W.N. & Meyer, A.D. (1989) Impact of therapeutic management on use of seclusion and restraint with disruptive adolescent inpatients. *Hospital and Community Psychiatry*, **40**, 3, 280–285.

47. LaVigna, G.W., Willis, T.J. & Donnellan, A.M. (1989) The role of positive programming in behavioural treatment. In Cipani, E. (Ed.) *The Treatment of Severe Behaviour Disorders. Behaviour Analysis Approaches* (pp. 59–83). Washington: American Association on Mental Retardation.

48. Lehmann, L.S., Padilla, M., Clark, S. & Loucks, S. (1983) Training personnel in the prevention and management of behaviour. *Hospital and Community Psychiatry*, 34, 1, 40–43.

49. MacIntyre, D. (1999) *MacIntyre Undercover. One Man, Four Lives*. London: BBC.

50. Martin, L.S. (1999) Nursing home uses skills lab to determine impact of Nonviolent Crisis Intervention. *Journal of Safe Management of Disruptive and Assaultive Behaviour*, 7, 4, 12–13.

51. McDonnell, A. (1997) Training care staff to manage challenging behaviour: An evaluation of a three day training course. *British Journal of Developmental Disabilities*, 43, 2, 85, 156–162.

52. McDonnell, A. & Jones, P. (undated) *Staff training in the management of aggressive behaviours: Outcome data on 15 training courses*.

53. McDonnell, A. & Reeves, S. (1996) Phasing out seclusion through staff training and support. *Nursing Times*, **92**, 32, 43–44.

54. McDonnell, A., & Sturmey, P. (2000) The social validation of physical restraint procedures with people with developmental disabilities: a comparison of young people and professional groups. *Research in Developmental Disabilities*, 21, 85–92.

55. McDonnell, A., Sturmey, P. & Deaden (1993) The acceptability of physical restraint procedures for people with a learning difficulty. *Behavioural and Cognitive Psychotherapy*, **21**,255–264.

56. McGowan, S., Wynaden, D., Harding, N. Yassine, A. & Parker, J. (1999) Staff confidence in dealing with aggressive patients: A benchmarking exercise. *Australian and New Zealand Journal of Mental Health Nursing*, **8**, 104–108.

57. Miles, D. (1999) *Preventing and responding to aggression. An evaluation of this major training programme and its impact on learning disability services.* Bristol: Bristol Social Services.

58. Mortimer, A. (1995) Reducing violence on a secure ward. *Psychiatric Bulletin*, **19**, 605–608.

59. Murphy, G., Estien, D. & Clare, I.C.H. (1996) Services for people with intellectual disabilities and challenging behaviour. *Journal of Applied Research in Intellectual Disabilities*, **9**, 256–283.

60. Murray, G.C., McKenzie, K., Quigley, A. & Sinclair, B. (1999) The relationship between training and the experience of aggression in the workplace in residential care staff working in learning disability services. *Journal for Learning Disabilities for Nursing, Health and Social Care*, **3**, 4, 214–218.

61. Nethell, G. (1999) *Service Evaluation. Breakaway and minimal restraint training.* Bridgend: Clinical Psychology Department, Bro Morgannwg NHS Trust.

62. Nunno, M.A., Holden, M.J. & Leidy, B. (In press) Evaluating and monitoring the impact of a crisis intervention system on a residential child care facility. *Children and Youth Services Review.*

63. Parkes, J. (1996) Control and restraint training: a study of its effectiveness in a medium secure unit. *Journal of Forensic Psychiatry*, 7, 3, 525–534

64. Paterson, B., Turnbull, J. & Aitken, I. (1992) An evaluation of a training course in the short-term management of violence. *Nurse Education Today*, **12**, 368–375.

65. Paterson, B. (1998) Restraint and sudden death from asphyxia. *Nursing Times*, **94**,44, 62–64.

66. Pollanen, M.S., Chiasson, D.A., Cairns, J.T., & Young, J.G. (1998) Unexpected death related to restraint for excited delirium: a retrospective study of deaths in police custody and in the community. *Canadian Medical Association Journal*, **158**, 12, 1603–1607.

67. Phillips, D. & Rudestam, K.E. (1995) Effect of non-violent self-defense training on male staff members' aggression and fear. *Psychiatric Services*, **46**, 2, 164–168.

68. Rangecroft, M.E.H, Tyrer, S.P. & Berney, T.P. (1994) The use of seclusion and emergency medication in a hospital for people with learning disability. *British Journal of Psychiatry*, **170**, 273–277.

69. Rice, M.E., Helzel, M.F., Varney, G.W. & Quinsey, V.L. (1985) Crisis prevention and intervention training for psychiatric hospital staff. *American Journal of Community Psychology*, **13**, 3, 289–304.

70. Roggla, M., Wagner, A., Muellner, M., Bur, A., Roggla, H., Hirschl, M.M. & Roeggla, G. (1997) Cardiorespiratory consequences to hobble restraint. *Wiener Klinische Wochenscrift*, **109**, 10, 359–361.

71. Rosenthal, T.L., Edwards, N.B., Rosenthal, R.H. & Ackerman, B.J. (1992) Hospital violence: site, severity, and nurses' preventive training. *Issues in Mental Health Nursing*, **13**, 349–356.

72. Royal College of Psychiatrists (1995) *Strategies for the management of disturbed and violent patients in psychiatric units.* Council Report CR41. London: Royal College of Psychiatrists.

73. Sailas, E. & Fenton, M. (1999) Seclusion and restraint for serious mental illness. *Cochrane Database of Systematic Reviews*, **4**.

74. Smoot, S.L. & Gonzales, J.L. (1995) Cost-effective communication skills training for state hospital employees. *Psychiatric Services*, **46**, 8, 819–822.

75. Standing Nursing and Midwifery Committee (1999) *Mental Health Nursing: "Addressing Acute Concerns".* London: SNMAC.

76. Spreat, S., Lipinski, D.P., Hill, J., & Halpin, M. (1986) Safety indices associated with the use of contingent restraint procedures. *Applied Research in Mental Retardation*, 7, 475–481.

77. Stirling, C. & McHugh, A. (1998) Developing a non-aversive intervention strategy in the management of aggression and violence for people with learning disabilities using natural therapeutic holding. *Journal of Advanced Nursing*, **27**, 503–509.

78. St.Thomas' Psychiatric Hospital, Ontario, Canada (1976) A program for the prevention and management of disturbed behaviour. *Hospital and Community Psychiatry*, **27**, 724–727.

79. Sturmey, P. (1999) Correlates of restraint use in an institutional population. *Research in Developmental Disabilities*, **20**, 5, 339–346.

80. Thackrey, M. (1987) Clinician confidence in coping with patient aggression: assessment and enhancement. *Professional Psychology: Research and Practice*, **18**, 1, 57–60.

81. Titus, R. (1989) Therapeutic crisis intervention training. *Journal of Child and Youth Care*, **4**, 61–71.

82. Van Den Pol, R.A, Reid, D.H. & Fuqua, R.W. (1983) Peer training of safety-related skills to institutional staff: benefits for trainers and trainees. *Journal of Applied Behaviour Analysis*, **16**, 139–156.

83. Welsh Health Planning Forum (1992) *Protocol for investment in health gain: Mental Handicap (Learning Disabilities).* Cardiff: Welsh Office/ NHS Directorate

84. Whittington, R., Shuttleworth, S. & Hill, L. (1996) Violence to staff in a general hospital setting. *Journal of Advanced Nursing*, **24**, 326–333.

85. Wing, J., Marriott, S., Palmer, C. & Thomas, T. (1998) *Management of Imminent Violence. Clinical practice guidelines to support mental health services.* Occasional Paper OP41. London: Royal College of Psychiatrists.

86. Wright, S. (1999) Physical restraint in the management of violence and aggression in in-patient settings: A review of issues. *Journal of Mental Health*, **8**, 5, 459–472.

Appendix – Sample Measures

Measure 1:   Multiple Choice Knowledge – Guidelines & Questionnaire

Measure 2:   Confidence Scale

Measure 3:   Training Feedback Form

Measure 4:   Assessing Competence in Physical Skills

Measure 5:   Measuring Direct Training Outcomes

Introduction

Examples of four measures for measuring direct training outcomes are presented on the following pages. They correspond to the minimum data set for trainers specified on page 34 and consist of:

- A Knowledge Questionnaire

- A Confidence Questionnaire

- A Feedback Form

- Notes on Assessing Physical Skills (together with two example task analyses)

Trainers can use the measures as templates for devising their own assessments; the confidence questionnaire should however be used as written because the measure has been utilised in a number of studies and appears to have reasonable psychometric properties.

In addition, a simple form for monitoring the indirect outcomes of training is provided, together with some illustrations of how the data from the form can be routinely used to produce a series of summary measures.

Measure 1: Multiple Choice Knowledge – Guidelines & Questionnaire

Source: New York State Office of Intellectual Disabilities (1988) Strategies for Crisis Intervention and Prevention. New York: NYOMRDD.

Reprinted with permission of the publishers.

I. Introduction

The Guidelines for "Strategies for Crisis Intervention and Prevention" training program requires annual renewal of certification "… upon successful completion of a written test on SCIP principles and demonstration of competency performance in the use of personal interventions." The written tests on SCIP should be developed locally.

In planning for written tests, instructors should answer certain questions before writing test items. The questions are:

1.   What proportion of all the items on the test should be written for each content area?

2.   What type of items are most appropriate to use?

3.   How long should the test be?

4.   How difficult should the test be?

The written test should be used as a mastery or a criterion-referenced test. The object of giving a written test is to ensure that each participant understands and is able to apply the material covered in the course. To assist instructors in the development of written tests, tips for test development and sample items are included here.

II. Tips for Writing Test Items

There are a number of different test items that can be used on a test. Two major categories of test item are:

- recall – students produce their own answers from memory

- recognition – students select answers from choices supplied by the test writer.

Examples of recall items are essay questions requiring an extended answer from students, the short-answer question requiring one or two sentences for an answer; and the completion item requiring only a word or phrase for an answer. Examples of recognition items include true-false statements, the multiple-choice item, and the matching item.

In training programs where time and ease of scoring are factors, the use of recognition items is advantageous. Tests using recognition items, the multiple-choice type has more pluses than does the matching or true-false. True-false items encourage guessing (50% choice) and are difficult to construct to test higher levels of learning.

Matching items are somewhat cumbersome, the tests take quite a bit of time to take, and they are not well suited to testing a large amount of different kinds of knowledge. All things considered, the well constructed multiple choice item is the most suitable test item to select. Regardless of the type of test items used to make up a written test, several points are important for development:

1. Avoid "trick" items which do nothing but waste time and confuse and frustrate the student

2. Avoid items that force the student to only recall facts.

3. Tests should be fair. Questions should relate only to the material the student should know.

4. Keep track of how often students miss specific test items. When half or more students miss a particular item, it is probably a poor question and needs to be reworded.

5. A good test should be easy to take and easy to score.

6. Include enough, but only enough, items on a test to fully assess the students' mastery of the objectives. A good rule of thumb is "at least one question per objective." Items should deal with important aspects of the curriculum.

7. Each item should be independent. The answer to one should not be required as a condition for solving another.

When writing multiple choice items, the following suggestions should be followed for better quality tests:

1. The stem of the item must clearly formulate a problem.

2. Include as much of the item as possible in the stem and keep options as short as possible.

3. Include in the stem only the material needed to make the problem clear and specific.

4. Use negatives (e.g. not) sparingly in the stem.

5. Use novel material in writing problems to measure understanding or application of principles.

6. There should be only one correct or clearly best answer.

7. Wrong choices must be plausible.

8. Avoid clues to the correct answers (e.g. grammatical inconsistency, length, "clang" associations)

9. Use the option "None of the above" only when the answer is classified unequivocally as right or wrong.

10. Avoid the use of "all of the above"

III. Sample Items

The following items have been developed as a resource in the development of written tests for Level II certification. They may be used as is, in modified form, or in conjunction with locally developed items.

SAMPLE MULTIPLE CHOICE QUESTIONS

For each of the following items, circle the letter of the response which best answers the question or which correctly completes the statement. Asterisks denote correct responses.

Awareness

1. *Policies regarding client protection hold staff responsible to prevent abuse of clients. These policies apply to:*

    A. Staff with client contact responsibilities

    B. Facility based staff

    C. Non-administrative titles

    D. Every employee regardless of status*

2. *Any employee witnessing or becoming aware of an incident of abuse must immediately:*

    A. Intercede to protect the client from injury or harm*

    B. Notify their supervisor

    C. Go about finishing their assigned tasks

    D. Call the safety department

3. *Policy indicates that if a client is injuring or attempting to injure self or others:*

    A. Staff must attempt to intervene regardless of level of training*

    B. Only certified staff are allowed to intervene

    C. Only safety officers are allowed to use physical interventions

    D. Staff must wait until an injury occurs before intervening

4. *An element of an effective staff training program would include:*

    A. Strategies that are non-personal, non-judgemental, and non-punitive

    B. It strives to develop a co-ordinated approach

    C. It be in accord with basic principles of a proactive approach

    D. All of the above*

5. *The SCIP program is intended to develop skills:*

    A. For crisis teams only

    B. For each individual staff member*

    C. For secure units

    D. For non-community based programs

6. *A disadvantage to using physical restraint devices such as straight jackets is:*

    A. The client loses control of his/her own behaviour

    B. Physical restraint devices are difficult for staff to apply

    C. Physical restraint devices present certain health risks such as an elevation in blood pressure

    D. The straight jacket can become a convenience to staff and can be used to threaten the client to be good

    E. All of the above*

7. *An advantage to using medication to control aggressive behaviour is:*

    A. The medication controls the aggressive behaviour and also slows down many of the client's reflexes in the body

    B. It can calm an individual down enough to allow them to engage in normal daily activities with little or no aggressive behaviours*

C. Medications can cause a number of side effects, some of which are irreversible

D. Medications can postpone the problem rather than deal with it

8. *Which of the following statements is true according to Client Protection Policies?*

A. Punishment can be used routinely by staff to stop aggressive behaviours on the part of a client

B. An aggressive client can be put into seclusion to calm down

C. Staff may spank a client to correct an aggressive behaviour if the client is under 21

D. Obscene language directed to a client by a staff member is considered verbal abuse*

9. *According to the SCIP program, the best way to deal with aggressive behaviours whenever possible is by using:*

A. Medications

B. Client specific interventions*

C. Physical restraint devices

D. Lobotomies

10. *If a staff person is not trained in SCIP, what should he/she do if an assault of a client or staff takes place in his/her presence?*

A. As appropriate, render assistance to stop assault*

B. Leave the area immediately

C. Utilise a one person take down

D. If not trained, cannot intervene

11. *Which of the following is New York State Office of Mental Retardation and Developmental Disabilities' approved programme for training staff in a sequential process for crisis prevention and intervention?*

A. Strategies for Crisis Intervention and Prevention (SCIP)*

B. Gentle Art of Self Defence

C. Non-violent Approach to Physical and Psychological Intervention (NAPPI)

D. Crisis Prevention Institute (CPI)

Understanding

12. *Which of the following are characteristics which may increase the likelihood that a developmentally disabled individual will react inappropriately in stressful situations?*

    A. Excellent organisational skills

    B. Short frustration tolerance and poor impulse control*

    C. Good sense of humour and good communication skills

    D. Excessive creativity and clarity of thought

13. *As a staff person involved in a situation where there is potential for aggressive behaviour, which of the following factors is most likely to increase the chances that aggressive behaviour will occur?*

    A. Your unrealistic expectations of the client*

    B. Today is pay day

    C. Team meeting is scheduled for tomorrow

    D. Your spouse has just received an award

14. *Regardless of anyone's disability,*

    A. All disabled people should be treated the same

    B. All persons should be restrained

    C. Everyone needs to be institutionalised

    D. All persons can learn and grow*

15. *Which of the following could be an environmental causative factor for disruptive behaviour?*

    A. Need for attention

    B. Crowding*

    C. Fatigue

    D. Illness

16. *If an individual client lacks an appropriate means for emotional release, which one of the following is a step for staff to take to avoid potential problems?*

    A. Teach appropriate ways to express anger*

    B. Never expect anger in any situation

C. Encourage total restraint of anger

D. Punish anger immediately after it happens

17. *When agitated behaviour is paired with crying or when a person seems unable to calm down from agitation:*

A. Call the ambulance for transport to a hospital

B. It is possible that pain or illness is the cause*

C. Write a daily note indicating behaviour

D. Restrain the person until crying stops

18. *Inability to communicate needs can lead to severe frustration. One step to take to help alleviate poor communication skills is to:*

A. Teach alternative forms of communication*

B. Ignore any attempts at communication

C. Use a tape recorder to record communication attempts

D. Call for a speech therapist at each communication attempt

19. *One characteristic of most developmentally delayed individuals which may add to levels of frustration is:*

A. Decreased ability to understand the environment*

B. Increased activity level

C. Feelings of superiority

D. Excessive confidence in any situation

20. *One thing that can be said about developmentally delayed individuals is they:*

A. Are never on time

B. Have shorter than average life expectancy

C. Are never able to gain control over their behaviour

D. Are more similar to normal people than they are different*

21. *The emphasis on staff working with clients who display aggressive behaviour should always be to:*

A. Control behaviours all of the time

B. Assist individuals in developing self control*

C. Seek shelter whenever aggressive behaviour occurs

D. Ignore all aggressive behaviour

Calming

22. *When a personal intervention technique is used on an emergency basis, which one of the following applies?*

A. The technique is only to be used until the client is calm*

B. The technique is used for a minimum of 20 minutes

C. Personal interventions should not be used for emergencies

D. Use a takedown first, ask questions later

23. *A personal intervention must be terminated immediately if the following should occur.*

1. Client shows a sudden change of colour

2. Client has difficulty breathing

3. Client vomits

4. Client says he or she is calm

A. 1,2 and 3 but not 4*

B. 1,2 and 4 but not 3

C. 1,3 and 4 but not 2

D. 2,3 and 4 but not 1

24. *Which of the following apply during a lying wrap-up?*

1. An open airway passage must be ensured

2. Excessive weight and pressure must not be applied to the client's back and neck

3. Should take place on a firm surface not a couch or a bed

4. Should use as much force as necessary to control the client

A. 1,2 and 3 but not 4*

B. 1,2 and 4 but not 3

C. 1,3 and 4 but not 2

D. 2,3 and 4 but not 1

25. *If a client is held in a wrap-up, a supervisor is to be notified within what period of time?*

    A.   Twenty minutes*

    B.   Thirty minutes

    C.   Fifty minutes

    D.   One hour

26. *Which of the following are to be considered in attempting to prevent a crsisis:*

    1.   Use early signs of agitation to teach and encourage coping skills

    2.   Avoid unnecessary confrontations

    3.   Use non-verbal and/or verbal calming techniques

    4.   Use a takedown and lying wrap-up

    A.   1,2 and 3 but not 4*

    B.   1,2 and 4 but not 3

    C.   1,3 and 4 but not 2

    D.   2,3 and 4 but not 1

27. *When should an intrusive personal intervention such as a takedown or lying wrap-up be used?*

    A.   To interrupt or terminate a truly dangerous situation*

    B.   As a punishment for a misbehaviour

    C.   As a technique to maintain control

    D.   As a method of demonstrating authority.

Prevention

28. *If a takedown or lying wrap-up is to be included as part of a behaviour plan, which of the following apply:*

    1.   The behaviour plan is written by a psychologist

    2.   Other less intrusive techniques must have been tried first

    3.   The behaviour plan has been reviewed and approved by the client's Interdisciplinary Team

    A.   1,2 and 3*

B.   2 and 3 but not 1

C.   3 and 1 but not 2

29–32   *Read the following description and respond to the accompanying questions as they relate to Philip.*

Philip is a 24-year-old individual with severe mental retardation who attends a day training program, and is working at the prevocational level. He can understand simple two step directions, and can make his basic wants and needs known through two-three word phrases and gestures. Philip is ambulatory but has an awkward gait. He also has epilepsy with occasional seizure activity; as a result he has to wear a helmet daily. He has severe mood swings which result in his seeming to enjoy social contact at times and rejecting it at others. He seems to prefer to work with female staff members. He also has an old sweatshirt which he wears every day. In the day training program, Philip works very well with his supervisor Mary. He is usually cooperative and works well with other clients. One day, Mary is out of work because of illness. Joe replaces Mary as Philip's supervisor for the day. One of the first things Joe does is to ask Philip to remove his old sweatshirt. Philip refuses and responds by screaming "No" and yelling loudly.

29.   *In the situation just described, what are some warning signs of potentially disruptive behaviour?*

A.   Mary is absent*

B.   Philip has an awkward gait

C.   Philip uses gestures to make his needs known

D.   Joe is older than Mary

30.   *What non-verbal calming techniques could Joe use with Philip?*

A.   Eye contact, touch control, body position*

B.   Humour, reassurance, counselling

C.   Wrestling, tackling, pushing

D.   Teasing, yelling, sarcasm

31.   *If calming techniques do not work with Philip and he becomes aggressive what personal intervention techniques could be employed that would be least restrictive?*

A.   Blocking punches, one person escort*

B.   One person takedown, lying wrap-up

C.   Full nelson arm lock

D.   Choke hold, pressure points

32.   *It now seems that Mary will be gone for over three months because of her illness. Joe believes that something must be done to help Philip change his aggressive behaviour. As a member of the planning team in the day program what would you recommend be done to decrease Philip's aggressive behaviour?*

A.   Develop programs to encourage more positive behaviour while discouraging aggressive behaviour*

B.   Move Philip to a different program until Mary returns to work.

C.   Give Philip medications to help control his behaviour

D.   Have Joe transfer to a different program and find a new supervisor for Philip.

Measure 2: Confidence Scale

Source: Thackrey, M. (1987) Clinician confidence in coping with patient aggression: assessment and enhancement. *Professional Psychology: Research and Practice*, 18, 1, 57–60. (Also used in studies 4 and 54).

Copyright © 1987 by the American Psychological Association. Reprinted with permission.

Confidence in Coping with Patient Aggression Instrument

Please rate each of the following ten statements by placing a circle around the number which best describes how you feel at the moment. Please make sure that you answer every question.

1. *How comfortable are you working with an aggressive patient?*

Very Uncomfortable   Very Comfortable

0   1   2   3   4   5   6   7   8   9   10

2. *How good is your present level of training for handling psychological aggression?*

Very Poor   Very Good

0   1   2   3   4   5   6   7   8   9   10

3. *How able are you to intervene physically with an aggressive patient?*

Very Unable   Very Able

0   1   2   3   4   5   6   7   8   9   10

4. *How self-assured do you feel in the presence of an aggressive patient?*

Not very self-assured   Very self-assured

0   1   2   3   4   5   6   7   8   9   10

5. *How able are you to intervene psychologically with a patient?*

Very Unable   Very Able

0   1   2   3   4   5   6   7   8   9   10

6. *How good is your present level of training for handling physical aggression?*

Very Poor   Very Good

0   1   2   3   4   5   6   7   8   9   10

7. *How safe do you feel around an aggressive service user?*

Very Unsafe   **Very Safe**

0   1   2   3   4   5   6   7   8   9   10

8. *How effective are the techniques that you know for dealing with aggression?*

Very Ineffective   **Very Effective**

0   1   2   3   4   5   6   7   8   9   10

9. *How able are you to meet the needs of an aggressive patient?*

Very Unable   **Very Able**

0   1   2   3   4   5   6   7   8   9   10

10. *How able are you to protect yourself physically from a patient?*

Very Unable   **Very Able**

0   1   2   3   4   5   6   7   8   9   10

N.B. Allen & Tynan (2000) changed the term 'patient' to 'service user' without having any adverse effect on the internal consistency of the scale.

Measure 3: Training Feedback Form

Source: Intensive Support Service (1999) *Positive Behaviour Management Training Manual*. Cardiff: Welsh Centre for Learning Disabilities

Training Evaluation Form

Date (s) of Training:

Venue:

Trainers:

1. *How effective was this event in meeting your personal learning needs?*

    Very ineffective   1   2   3   4   5   Very effective

2. *Do you feel that the training will help you work more effectively with service users who show aggressive behaviours?*

    Not at all   1   2   3   4   5   Very much so

3. *Do you feel more confident about working with aggressive behaviours as a result of the training?*

    Not at all   1   2   3   4   5   Very much so

4. *Do you think that you will be able to apply the physical interventions that you have been taught in the workplace?*

    Not at all   1   2   3   4   5   Very much so

5. *How relevant were the moves that you were taught?*

    Not at all   1   2   3   4   5   Very much so

6. *Do you think that you will have trouble recalling the moves that you have been taught?*

    Not at all   1   2   3   4   5   Very much so

7. *How appropriate was the venue for this event?*

    Very appropriate   1   2   3   4   5   Very inappropriate

8.   *How appropriate was the balance between preventative and reactive interventions?*

Very satisfactory   1   2   3   4   5   Very unsatisfactory

9.   *Were there any things that you had hoped to learn from the course but that were not covered?*

_____

_____

_____

_____

_____

10.   *Were there any parts of the training that you felt could have been omitted without detracting from the overall value of the course?*

_____

_____

_____

_____

_____

Thank you for your help

Measure 4: Assessing Competence in Physical Skills

The ability of trainers to teach physical skills and to assess the competence of participants in behaviour management training will vary as a function of the following factors:

1.   Trainer: trainee ratio

2.   Number of moves to be taught

3.   Complexity of moves to be taught

Simply stated, the greater the volume and complexity of moves to be taught, the higher the ratio of trainers to trainees that will be required. The level of assessment in physical interventions will also vary according to the nature of the training being provided. In training trainers courses, for example, it is likely that a far higher demonstration of physical competence will be required than when training direct care staff. Additional skills (teaching ability, presentational skills, interpersonal skills, group management skills etc.) will also need to be assessed in trainer training.

In cases where trainer:trainee ratios prohibit the assessment of each individual participant on each move taught, a more global rating of competence may be all that is possible. Where more detailed individualised assessment is practicable, task analysis of moves should provide the basis for participant assessment.

Task Analysis & Physical Interventions

Task analysis is a process by which a physical skill or action is broken down into its component responses. Each response represents a behaviour (or step) that must be performed if the skill is to be correctly completed. It is a particularly appropriate technique for analysing and teaching physical intervention skills.

The following guidelines are offered in terms of constructing a task analysis:

- Perform the move in exactly the way that participants will be required to perform it

- Break the move down into its component steps and list them in the order in which they will be performed. Video taping the move will aid this analysis

- Try to identify functional response units – these are observable changes in the move being performed

- For each step, specify the discrete, measurable actions that must be fulfilled for the step to be successfully completed. This helps ensure that there is no ambiguity between correct and incorrect performance – the move is either performed correctly or incorrectly

- Try to write the task analysis so that steps are of roughly the same size and can be presented in the form of a simple instruction

- Training in physical interventions should aim for *topographically correct* performance – that is, participants complete the move in exactly the way shown. *Functionally correct* performance – where participants reach the correct endpoint but not by using the method specified – is unhelpful in physical intervention training

- Task analyses for training in physical intervention skills should try to avoid or minimise judgmental steps that do not specify observable behaviours and which therefore involve a range of correctness. Accurate performance is hard to assess with judgmental steps, and appropriate performance under stress is likely to prove problematic. The problem with judgmental steps is well illustrated in the following quote that refers to a fairly standard approach to responding to bites:

  ". . . in relation to a situation where a child bites a worker, 'the adult gently pushes her arm toward the child, into the bite'. Anyone who has experienced the excruciating pain of a bite might be forgiven for assuming that to 'gently' do anything is superhuman' (Heron, 1996, p. 11)

- Complex moves will need to be broken down into smaller steps. Be aware that the more complex a move is to perform, the harder it will be to teach, the more difficult it will be for participants to retain, and the less likely they will be able to perform it adequately in the field when under pressure

- Key steps should be subject to massed practice – the steps concerned should be practiced repeatedly until accomplished and before moving onto the next part of the move

- Once accomplished, different steps within complex moves should be linked (or chained) together to form the complete move

- Set criteria for successful performance of the move. In physical intervention training, this will typically require the correct performance of each step.

Two examples of task analysis now follow. The first example (from Van den Pol et al, 1983) is a fairly global analysis of a set of self-protective skills used in a role play test. This is followed by a more specific task analysis for a single breakaway technique:

Example 1: Global Task Analysis: Component steps for a self-defense procedure

1. Staff member (S) stands within reach of resident (R) within 5 secs of hit

2. S states R's name and instructs incompatible response within 10 sec of hit

3. S physically prompts desired response within 10 sec of instruction or within 20 sec of hit

4. S blocks punch with same-side arm, with hand fisted (thumb contacting fingers) and using forearm (between wrist and elbow joint)

5. S blocks kick by raising same-side leg 6 inches with foot partially occluding support leg and torso turning approximately 90° to the side

6. S releases clothing grab by thumb pry within 5 sec of grab

7. S releases body part grab by thumb or rotating out within 5 sec of grab

8. S lifts and holds chair between self and R's chair within 5 sec of attack

9 S states criteria for use of self-defense technique as per policy: to protect people (any) and property

Example 2: Specific task Analysis – Single-handed arm grab

Step – Trainee should:	Performance (circle response)
Adopt the correct stance (side on stance, front foot pointing towards assailant, rear foot at an angle of approximately 60% to front foot)	Correct/incorrect
Clench the fist of the arm being held	Correct/incorrect
Bend the elbow of the arm being held to approximately 90%	Correct/incorrect
Using their body weight, pull the arm being held between the fingers and thumb of the assailant's grip	Correct/incorrect
Bring the released arm outwards and across their own body	Correct/incorrect
Increase space between themselves and the the assailant to at least two arm's length	Correct/incorrect
Reassume the correct stance	Correct/incorrect

Measure 5: Measuring Direct Training Outcomes

The following form provides a simple recording procedure for monitoring the usage of reactive behavioural procedures. A series of example analyses then follow; the graphs shown only represent a sample of the analyses that are possible using this form.

The data provided are from a fictitious residential service for adults with learning disabilities and challenging behaviours before and after the staff attended a behaviour management course.

Figure 1 provides a simple comparison of pre-training and post training levels of behavioural incidents and restraint use. Both variables appear to have reduced from their baseline levels, although the reduction of restraint usage is greater than the reduction in levels of challenging behaviour, particularly in the immediate post-training period. In interpreting these data, their potential sensitivity to changes in both service user groups and staff groups must be borne in mind.

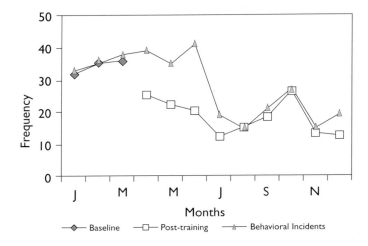

Fig. 1 Frequency of behavioural incidents and restraint use

The duration of restraint usage increased initially following training (Fig. 2), although the overall trend is decreasing. The initial increase may reflect greater vigilance in recording patterns following training. Longer-term recording will help clarify what actual trends are emerging. As required medication usage has clearly declined (Fig. 3); this is an important finding, as collateral increases in one form of reactive procedure (medication) might be expected as the usage of another reactive procedure (restraint) declines. The fact that both measures have declined perhaps validates the suggestion that the training has indeed had a positive effect.

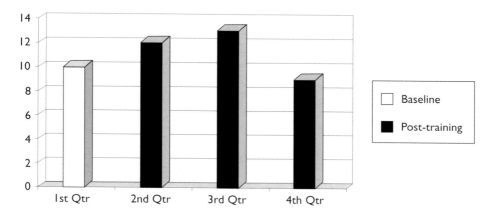

Fig. 2 Average duration of restraint use (in minutes)

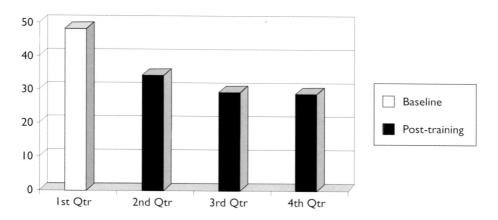

Fig. 3 Use of as required medication

The next two graphs (Figs. 4 & 5) suggest a different pattern of restraint usage across the course of the day and week. More restraint is used in the evening and at weekends. This may be due to decreased levels of active programming at these times, a higher density of service users being present, a lower ratio of staff: service users and so on. Investigation of these possibilities will allow appropriate organisational or programmatic adjustments to be made. The impact of these adjustments on the data can then be tracked.

Figures 6 and 7 show the relationship between restraint usage and individual service users and individual staff members. It is apparent that restraint is used far more with certain service users than others. This may be entirely appropriate, and in accordance with the different challenges that they present. A further analysis of these challenges in relationship to restraint use will allow this possibility to be checked. If these data do not indicate that increased restraint use is linked with increased severity and frequency of challenging behaviour, then further investigations would have to be made in order to identify what other variables are determining the need for restraint usage.

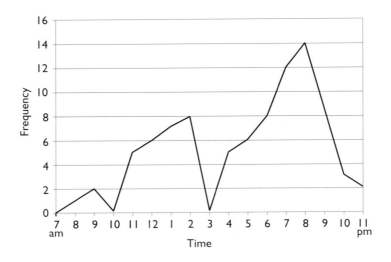

Fig. 4 Restraint use by time of day

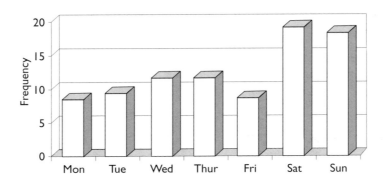

Fig. 5 Restraint use by days of the week

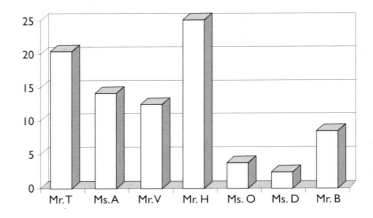

Fig. 6 Use of restraint by service user

Similar issues arise out of the staff graph (Fig. 7). Some staff are more involved in restraint than others. This may reflect variations in training received, confidence levels or competence levels. Less confident staff tend to rely on more confident staff in crisis situations. Alternatively, maybe the staff concerned initiate restraint too readily. Again, further investigations would be required here.

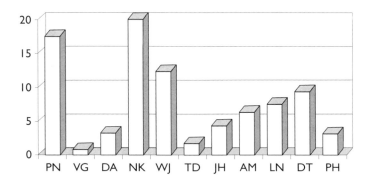

Fig. 7 Staff implementing restraint

Rates of injuries to both users and staff have declined (Figs. 8 & 9). These graphs record frequency only. The additional data on the form concerning actions that needed to be taken with regard to dealing with injuries would also allow a crude assessment to be made as to whether the nature and severity of injuries had altered.

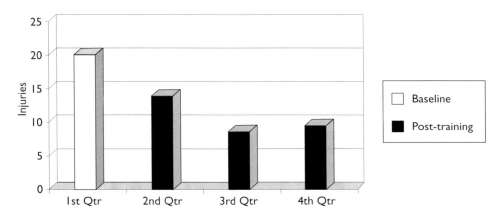

Fig. 8 Rates of service user injuries

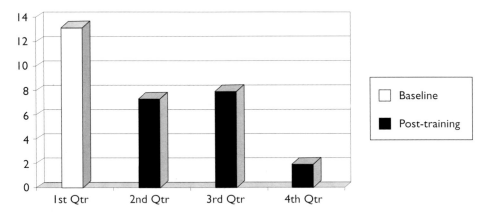

Fig. 9 Injuries to staff

Figure 10 shows the overall pattern of reactive strategy usage. As would be hoped, most carer responses have focused on distraction and defusion strategies. Removal procedures are the next most frequently used procedures, followed in order by breakaways and restraint.

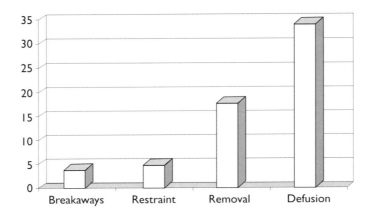

Fig. 10 Overall reactive strategies employed

The recording of the specific physical interventions used allows a comparison to be made between what was taught on the training course that staff attended and what they use in practice (Fig. 11). Only approximately 30% of what was taught was actually used in the workplace. These data will allow the training to be reduced in scope at refresher sessions. This in turn will help the staff to retain more of the skills taught.

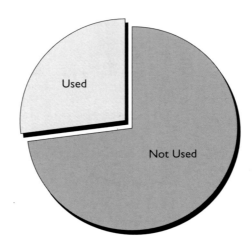

Fig. 11 Ratio of physical interventions taught to physical interventions used

REACTIVE STRATEGY MONITORING FORM

1. Service user name:

_____

2. Day & date of incident:

_____

3. Time of incident:

_____

4. Location of incident:

_____

5. Staff members involved:

_____

_____

6. Nature of reactive strategies employed (NB Please name any physical strategies employed):

_____

_____

Distraction/defusion:

_____

_____

Breakaways (specify):

_____

_____

Removal (specify):

_____

_____

Restraint (specify):

_____

_____

7. Specify the duration of any restraint procedures used:

_____

_____

8. Was as required medication given?

_____

_____

9. Specify any injuries to the service user and any necessary medical treatment:

_____

_____

10. Specify any injuries to staff and any necessary medical treatment:

_____

_____

11. Specify any potential implications for the service user's proactive and reactive care plans identified by the incident:

_____

_____

12. Completed by (name & date):

_____

13. Witnessed by (name & date):

_____

14. Copies forwarded to:

_____

bild Publications

The following titles may also be of interest to you. Please call 01562 850251 for a free copy of the latest publications catalogue.

- Physical Interventions: A Policy Framework
  John Harris, David Allen, Marion Cornick, Alan Jefferson and Richard Mills

This publication, in collaboration with the National Autistic Society, sets out the issues which services should address when developing policies around the use of physical restraint. It includes draft policy statements, examples of good and poor practice and practical suggestions for implementation.

£15.00, 1996, ISBN 1 873791 32 1

- The BILD Code of Practice for Trainers in the use of Physical Interventions

This publication provides guidance on current best practice for physical interventions training, based on consultation with trainers, DoH, DfEE and the Health and Safety Executive. The Code is an important reference document for commissioners of training and trainers themselves. It includes guidance on: policies; best interest criteria; techniques for physical intervention; health and safety; course organisation; monitoring performance; evaluation and record-keeping; professional conduct.

£8.00, 2001, ISBN 1 902519 78 7

- Easy Guide to the Human Rights Act
  Andrea Hughes and Phil Coombs

The Easy Guide to the Human Rights Act outlines the key elements of the Human Rights Act – and shows how they can be applied in daily life. The guide includes real life stories and examples to illustrate various abuses of human rights, as well as suggestions for good practice and contact details for more information. A free poster accompanying the guide lists the most important human rights and abuses of human rights, and can be used in day centres, residential homes, offices and clubs.

£8.00, 2001, ISBN 1 902519 75 2

To order any of these titles, please ring Plymbridge Distributors on 01752 202301. Please add 5% for postage and packing.